BRITISH INDEPENDENT BUSES IN THE 1980S

RICHARD STUBBINGS

AMBERLEY

First published 2019

Amberley Publishing
The Hill, Stroud
Gloucestershire, GL5 4EP

www.amberley-books.com

Copyright © Richard Stubbings, 2019

The right of Richard Stubbings to be identified as the Author of this work has been asserted in accordance with the Copyrights, Designs and Patents Act 1988.

ISBN 978 1 4456 8601 1 (print)
ISBN 978 1 4456 8602 8 (ebook)

All rights reserved. No part of this book may be reprinted or reproduced or utilised in any form or by any electronic, mechanical or other means, now known or hereafter invented, including photocopying and recording, or in any information storage or retrieval system, without the permission in writing from the Publishers.

British Library Cataloguing in Publication Data.
A catalogue record for this book is available from the British Library.

Typesetting by Aura Technology and Software Services, India. Printed in the UK.

Introduction

Independent operators come in all shapes and sizes. Over the years they have ranged from very small firms, with maybe just one vehicle or with very few, to large concerns with fleets numbering into the hundreds. A lot of their fleets have at times often contained a bewildering variety of vehicle and body types, some quite venerable in age, while others have been heavily standardised with the most modern vehicles available. Their operations have been similarly mixed, ranging from purely local private hires, with maybe a schools service or two as well, to regular, frequent long-distance express services and long-distance and continental touring. Some have operated intensive bus services serving major centres of population and inter-urban routes, while others have maybe just maintained a weekly market day-only service.

This book, illustrated with photographs from my own collection, is an attempt to show a selection of these operators and their vehicles through the turbulent decade of the 1980s. I say turbulent as it was the decade of two separate Transport Acts, one in 1980 and one in 1985, which brought about far-reaching changes to bus and coach services. The 1980 Act deregulated coach services and allowed local authorities to deregulate bus services on a trial basis, although in practice only about three areas trialled this deregulation of bus services as an experiment. The example of Hereford became well-known as small independent operators challenged the incumbent operator, Midland Red. A number of these new companies did not in fact last very long. The 1985 Act deregulated bus services in Great Britain and abolished road service licensing and allowed competition on local bus services for the first time in many years. All an operator was required to do was to give fifty-six days' notice to the Traffic Commissioner of their intention to start, cease or alter a service. The bus services operated by public organisations such as the National Bus Company were to be transferred to the private sector, with the exception of London. This resulted in the NBC being broken up and sold off, frequently to management buy-outs in the short term. Additionally, municipally owned companies were required to be changed into arms-length organisations. The big Passenger Transport Executives had to sell their bus fleets to private operators. By the end of the 1980s, the NBC and the PTEs were no more and what municipal companies there were existed as separate entities.

Prior to these two Acts, the NBC, the PTEs and the municipal companies worked in their areas, sometimes working jointly, and the independent operators worked in their areas. The PTEs controlled all the services within their own area as regards timetabling and fares. So how did all this change affect the independent operator? In many cases, after these two Acts these companies simply carried on in more or less the same way they always had. Others took the opportunity to expand existing operations and develop their services, sometimes stepping in to fill gaps left by the withdrawal of the former NBC operator. Other firms decided to try their hand at running bus services – something either completely new to them or that they had not done for many years – with varying degrees of success.

An early example of privatisation and the resulting competition in the world of express coach travel came after the 1980 Act with the formation of British Coachways. This was a group of companies that got together and set up a number of express coach services to directly compete with National Express. Some well-known names, such as Wallace Arnold, Shearings and Barton were involved, and a patriotic livery of red, white and blue was introduced, although in practice a lot of the vehicles operated in their normal company colours. The venture was not a success and lasted barely two years. In 1982 Trathens of Yelverton in Devon set up their service to London from Cornwall, offering hostess service, speed and a high degree of comfort in high-specification double-deck coaches. National Express set up their Rapide service to compete with it. Eventually the two firms got together and jointly marketed the Rapide service.

As well as the expansion in the independent sector, there were other changes as well. Inevitably there are always firms that go out of business, for a variety of reasons. The 1980s saw a number of firms depart from the roads, some as a result of the changes brought about by the deregulation of services as they were unable to compete, others through merger or takeover by larger outfits and others simply through retirement or other reasons. While after the 1985 Act all the companies were technically private, or independent, I have, for the purposes of this book, taken independent to mean private and outside the former NBC, PTE or municipal companies – i.e. the traditional independent. In practice a large number of these newly privatised companies were quickly absorbed into a few large groupings. Some of the names that disappeared from our streets and lanes were well-known companies with long and proud histories. One such company, and one that I always had a soft spot for, was Premier Travel of Cambridge, whose vehicles I used to see on trips to Cambridge to visit my grandfather. They were sold to AJS Holdings in 1988. A firm with links to Premier Travel was Yelloway, who I saw regularly in the West Country on their express services from Rochdale and Leeds, as well as on those family visits to Cambridge. They ventured into local bus operation, with less than successful results, and their smart AEC coaches disappeared from our roads in 1988, with their express services being absorbed into the National Express network. Other well-known firms pictured in this book that disappeared included Gash of Newark, which was taken over by Lincolnshire Road Car, and Barton, which merged with Trent, both in 1989.

My interest in buses all started way back in the early 1960s when I was a small child, leaning over the garden wall of the curacy where we lived during my father's period as the curate of a church in Taunton, watching the local Western National buses pass by on town services. Small amounts of photography were done as I got older and this increased when the family moved to the south-east of England, near Guildford, in the mid-1970s. It was there I started to come into contact with independent bus operation to any real extent, with firms such as Safeguard, Tillingbourne and Blue Saloon. In addition, I also started coming across non-Bristol/ECW vehicles and various London types, which for someone used to only standard Tilling types was something of a novelty. I was now able to get out and do more photography, fitting it in around my studies and my instrumental practice sessions. This will, I hope, explain why there appears to be a bias towards operators in the South West and the South East; quite simply, this was because I happened to spend the greater part of my time in the south of England during this period. Other than a few family holidays to the Lake District, my opportunities to venture further north, or to Scotland or Wales, were very limited during this time.

As can be seen from the illustrations in this book, the variety of vehicles at this time was wide. The travelling public, maybe particularly on express coaches, were demanding a higher standard of vehicle: a vehicle that was quiet, with comfortable seats, toilet facilities and refreshments. There was a growing number of imported makes appearing on the roads, with Volvo being an obvious example. This is reflected in the pictures I have selected for this book. If there seems to be a large number of vehicles of any particular firm, then this is because they operated a particularly interesting mixed fleet. Where a photograph has been included of a vehicle at a bus rally this is because the vehicle concerned was a member of that particular company's operational fleet at that time. If there are photographs of a less than perfect standard then I have included them for their historical value.

The information contained on *Bus View*, produced by Busdata Computing Services, has proved invaluable as a reference for checking service dates and histories of a number of vehicles. I must also acknowledge the information on Wikipedia that also serves as an extremely useful reference point. I am also grateful to my partner Debs for reading everything through for me to ensure it all makes sense, and for being there and encouraging me on my photo trips!

Serving Guildford since 1926, Safeguard has remained in the hands of the same family to the present day. VPF 42M, a Leyland Leopard with a Willowbrook body, is seen here leaving Farnham Road bus station on the service to Park Barn. This vehicle subsequently moved to Somerset in 1982, working with Safeway of South Petherton. Later bus deliveries to Safeguard carried Duple Dominant bus bodies until the arrival of the Leyland Lynx.

After standardising for several years on Duple-bodied Leyland Leopards and Tigers for their service buses, Safeguard purchased four Leyland Lynxes in 1987 and 1988. Leyland Lynx E51 MMT, seen here leaving Guildford's Friary bus station on a local service to Park Barn on 1 November 1989, was the second example to enter service.

Safeguard has always been known for its smart, modern coach fleet, which operates a mixture of private hires, UK and overseas tours and school services. UTN 956Y, pictured here outside Safeguard's garage in Guildford, is a Leyland Tiger with a Plaxton Paramount 3500 body. It was purchased from Moordale of Newcastle in June 1985 and remained in the fleet until December 1987.

Blue Saloon started operating town services in Guildford in 1973 with a fleet of ex-London RF types. These were replaced in the mid to late 1970s and into the 1980s with Bristol LHs, both new and second-hand, with the first one arriving in 1975. In all, Blue Saloon operated about thirteen Bristol LHs over the years, all with either ECW bus bodies or Plaxton coach bodies. Fitted with the usual ECW body, CPD 131T was the last LH delivered new to the company, arriving in May 1979. It is pictured here on 1 November 1989 in Guildford's Friary bus station. By now Blue Saloon had started using the fleetname 'Hoppa-Shoppa' rather than the company name. Personally, I preferred the 'Blue Saloon' name ...

Blue Saloon purchased Leyland National UCO 43L from Plymouth City Transport in July 1980. At this time, Leyland Nationals in the fleets of independent operators, especially second-hand examples, were still relatively rare. Also fairly unusual was the use of the MAP-inspired 'Weyfarer' local identity by an independent operator. They were more widely used by the local NBC operators, particularly Alder Valley. UCO stayed in the fleet until early 1989.

Another second-hand purchase, in May 1988, was OFR 970M (formerly Blackpool Corporation 570), an AEC Swift fitted with Marshall bodywork. Also carrying the 'Hoppa-Shoppa' fleet name, it was photographed in Guildford bus station on 1 November 1989. It lasted in the fleet until October 1995.

Tillingbourne Bus was formed in about 1924 and served the village communities largely situated between Guildford, Cranleigh and Dorking. In later years it was to grow to operate services into Sussex, Hampshire and Berkshire as well. TBC 658, a Leyland Tiger with a Plaxton Paramount 3200 Express body, was purchased from Borehamwood Travel in April 1986, having started life as AEF 992Y in the fleet of Trimdon Motor Services in County Durham. It is seen here in Guildford bus station on 1 November 1989, awaiting departure for Dorking and Brockham.

JTM 109V, an AEC Reliance with Duple Dominant bus bodywork purchased in late 1979, was the last AEC bus built. Pictured here in North Street, Guildford, preparing to depart on service 448 to Cranleigh via Peaslake, this vehicle served with Tillingbourne and its associated company Metrobus until 1992. After periods with other companies, including London & Country, it now survives in preservation.

Tillingbourne's FOD 942Y is a rare Wadham Stringer Vanguard-bodied Dennis Dorchester with a seating capacity of sixty-one. It was one of two delivered in April 1983. The rural nature of Tillingbourne's operations around Guildford and the surrounding villages did not lend itself to double-decker operation, so high-capacity single-deckers were the order of the day. 942 is pictured in Guildford Friary bus station while working route 446 to Holmbury St Mary, a route that was discontinued in 1985. 942 was sold in 1999.

Photographed in their Wrecclesham Depot are Farnham Coaches YPB 832T and TBD 622N. YPB is a Bedford YMT with a Plaxton Supreme IV body and TBD is a Bedford YRT with a Willowbrook body purchased in March 1983 from United Counties, with whom I photographed it in Cambridge. It stayed in Farnham until 1986. Farnham Coaches was eventually taken over by Safeguard of Guildford. The name survives, but vehicles now carry Safeguard colours.

Pictured the same day as the Bedfords was FBP 242X, a Robin Hood-bodied Mercedes-Benz L508 bought new in 1982. It stayed in the fleet until 1984, when it passed to the neighbouring fleet of Gales in Haslemere.

Epsom Coaches was a long-established operator in Surrey, operating coach tours and private hires. Delivered in 1981, AGJ 344W, a Leyland Tiger with a Plaxton Supreme IV body, was one of five Tigers purchased before the company changed to Volvo chassis. It was photographed when almost new at King's Cross station.

Deregulation of bus services in 1986 led to Epsom Coaches successfully tendering for Surrey County Council bus routes, initially using vehicles from their coach fleet. However, seen here at Epsom Clock Tower while working a service to Epsom Hospital is D603 RGJ, one of five Bedford YMTs with Plaxton Derwent bodies purchased in 1987.

Seen at their Baughurst depot in Hampshire are Whites NWL 645M and NWL 647M, former City of Oxford Ford R1014s with Willowbrook bodies. Initially part of the Whites of Camberley firm, the Baughurst operation was sold to the Berks Bucks Bus Company in 1989.

Another member of the Whites fleet at Baughurst was SNX 852M, a very smart Bristol LHL6L with Plaxton Panorama Elite III body, purchased from Smith of Wilmcote in 1977.

Porters of Dummer, near Basingstoke, bought SOE 925H from West Midlands PTE in 1979. A Park Royal-bodied Daimler Fleetline, it originated with Birmingham City Transport as their 3925 and is seen here at the depot in Dummer in 1984. This long-established company ceased operating in 1987.

Taylor's Coaches of Sutton Scotney, near Andover, was the owner of DBC 190C, a former Leicester Corporation AEC Renown with an East Lancs body. This was one of two Renowns the company owned, the other being a former Nottingham vehicle.

The flagship of the Bere Regis fleet when delivered in 1975, along with its four sisters, JFX 232N was a Bedford YRT with a Plaxton Panorama Elite III body. It is seen here at the company's Dorchester depot in 1988. This company, with its distinctive brown livery, was a familiar and much-loved sight around the lanes of Dorset.

Bere Regis & District operated an extensive fleet in Dorset, connecting villages with nearby towns, often with just a weekly market day service. Vehicles used were often elderly coaches, with service buses entering the fleet in its later years. As the bus network declined, so private hire and tours took on more importance, and it is on such a duty that I photographed ENF 560Y in Weston-super-Mare on 16 August 1989. A Volvo B10M-61 with a Duple Dominant IV body, it was purchased from Smiths of Wigan.

Brutonian 217 UYC, seen here in Yeovil bus station on the service from Bruton, is a 1963 AEC Reliance with the last Harrington bus body built. It originated with the Hutchings & Cornelius fleet in South Petherton. It's a pity this vehicle never made it into preservation.

The delightfully named village of Piddlehinton in Dorset was home to R. J. Cuff, who operated a service to Yeovil. Seen here on 18 August 1989 is NCN 813L, a Bristol RELH6G with a Plaxton Elite Express III body. Formerly in the fleet of Northern General as its 5041, it was one of six REs operated by Cuff over the years.

Wake's of Sparkford was a major operator in the Yeovil area for many years, and here PWJ 497X, a Bedford YNT/Duple Dominant, is seen in Central Road, Yeovil, on its way to Shepton Mallet on 18 August 1989. It was purchased from Cowdrey of Gosport.

Seen parked in Taunton on 21 November 1989 was one of the smaller coaches in the Wake's fleet, OPS 550X. A Bedford YMQ/S with a Duple Dominant II Express body, it joined the fleet in 1986, migrating to Somerset from Mills of Baltasound on Orkney.

A visit to the Wake's depot at Sparkford in the summer of 1981 revealed a number of gems parked up awaiting their next duty. Here, YRV 140 was a 1962 Bedford SB5 with Duple Super Vega body new to Byng's of Portsmouth and bought in 1963. Parked next to it is 312 KYC, a similarly bodied Bedford SB1 that was new to Bowerman of Taunton in 1961 and also bought by Wake's in 1963. Vehicles like these were often the mainstays of small country operators well into the 1980s. I well remember riding on coaches like these on my way to away rugby matches from school!

The successor to the Duple Super Vega was the Duple Bella Vega, seen here on BYU 339B, a Bedford SB5 purchased by Wake's from Newbury of Maiden Bradley in 1979. It is seen here on that same summer 1981 visit while parked next to YRV 301, another Super Vega-bodied SB5, which was new to Byng's of Portsmouth and was bought by Wake's in 1963.

Parked a short distance away on that day, next to a badly damaged Vauxhall Viva, was FYC 126C. One of two Willowbrook-bodied Bedford VAM5s bought in 1965, it was used frequently on the main Yeovil to Shepton Mallet service.

Also present on that summer visit was Wake's newest coach, WYD 103W, a manual gearbox Leyland Leopard with a Duple Dominant II body. It was also the company's first heavyweight vehicle, having been primarily a Bedford operator.

Seen leaving Yeovil bus station for Crewkerne on 14 August 1989 is GUG 129N (formerly West Yorkshire 1450), a Leyland National in the fleet of Coleman of Yeovil, which traded as Yeovillian. Two Safeway Leyland Leopards can be seen in the background.

The attractive village of South Petherton was the home of Safeway Services. Seen here on 24 November 1989 is their RYA 676L, a Willowbrook-bodied Leyland Leopard, one of two they bought new.

Another picture of VPF 42M, seen having now moved from the Safeguard of Guildford fleet to Safeway of South Petherton. It is seen here leaving Yeovil for Crewkerne on 14 August 1989. Over the years Safeway purchased a number of vehicles from Safeguard.

Seen on stand in Yeovil bus station in summer 1986 while preparing for departure to Hinton St George is TYD 911W, another Safeway Leyland Leopard, this time with a Duple Dominant bus body.

Two of Safeway's coaches are pictured here in Bath on 22 November 1989. YYA 122X is a Leyland Leopard with Plaxton Supreme V body, while A983 NYC is a Leyland Tiger with Plaxton Paramount 3200 Express body.

Still employed in the fleet of Taylors of Tintinhull in the early '80s was CYD 724C, an AEC Reliance with a stylish Harrington Grenadier body that originated with the nearby Safeway fleet in South Petherton.

Stark, Harris & Doe of Kings Nympton in Devon, trading as Country Bus, operated this former Cynon Valley Bristol RESL6L with an ECW body. LTG 38L is seen in Honiton on 18 August 1989.

That visit to Honiton on 18 August 1989 also revealed AFJ 694T, a Country Bus Bristol LH with a Plaxton Supreme Express body. Formerly Western National 3133, it is seen laying over on the service from Axminster and Lyme Regis. Meanwhile, LRO 452L, a Plaxton Panorama Elite III-bodied Bedford YRQ, is also seen. Purchased from Stamp of Honiton in 1988, it originated in far-away Hertfordshire, with the fleet of Spanner & Walker of St Albans.

For its size, Country Bus had quite a varied fleet. Also parked in Honiton on 18 August 1989 were MMB 970P (formerly Crosville ENL 970), a dual-purpose Leyland National, and an MCW-bodied Leyland Fleetline OUC 33R (formerly London DMS 2033).

Another vehicle captured in Honiton on 18 August 1989 was this former Eastern Scottish Alexander-bodied Seddon Pennine 7, ESC 844S, seen having migrated south to the Red Bus Services fleet of Holladay, Clyst Honiton.

Tally Ho! Coaches of Kingsbridge in Devon is unique in that it is the only operator in the UK with an exclamation mark in its name. It has always operated a wide variety of vehicles, as this set of photographs will show. The summer of 1981 gave me an opportunity to visit this interesting operator at both its Kingsbridge and Ivybridge depots. Photographed at its Ivybridge depot is COD 925C, a Bedford VAL14 with rare Marshall bodywork.

Parked at their Kingsbridge depot are ex-Galpin of Plymouth KPB 111K, a Ford R226 with a Duple Viceroy body, and 146 HUO, a 1962 Bristol FLF6B that was formerly Western National 1983.

An interesting vehicle in the Tally Ho! fleet was JOD 856N, a Ford R1014 with a Duple Dominant Express body built to a 7-foot 6-inch width to help negotiate the narrow Devon lanes.

Other vehicles photographed during that 1981 visit to Tally Ho! included RPH 104L, a former London Country Bristol LHS6L with the usual ECW body. Bought in March 1981, this vehicle eventually emigrated to the North East in 1986, ending its days with Trimdon Motor Services. In the background GCS 165E, a former Western SMT Daimler Fleetline, can be seen.

Parked at the Ivybridge depot was 114CUF, former Southdown 114, a Marshall-bodied Leyland Leopard of 1963 that found its way to Tally Ho! via Western National, in whose fleet it was number 28.

Back at the Kingsbridge depot, CBK 512C, a Plaxton Embassy-bodied Bedford SB13, lasted in the fleet until 1982. This vehicle originated with Byng's of Portsmouth.

This Duple Midland-bodied Bedford VAS, EGA 833C, originated with MacBraynes in the north of Scotland, passing to Highland Omnibus on its demise. It eventually moved south to Galpin of Plymouth before joining Tally Ho!

LPB 239D, a Bedford VAL14 with a Duple Vega Major body, moved to the south-west of England in 1976 from Whites of Camberley. It was seen at the Kingsbridge depot during my one and only visit to Tally Ho! in 1981.

Another vehicle to find its way to Tally Ho! from Scotland was KUS 606E, an Alexander-bodied Leyland Atlantean. Formerly Glasgow LA 351, this vehicle lasted another year in Devon, being withdrawn in 1982.

Tally Ho! did buy new vehicles as well, including TOD 658R, a Plaxton Supreme-bodied Seddon Pennine 7, seen at the Ivybridge depot. New Pennine 7s were rare outside the Scottish Bus Group.

Ede of Par, near St Austell, was well known for its fondness for AEC Regent Vs, and also for purchasing vehicles from the AERE at Harwell. Here, 239 AJB is seen at the garage in Par, together with CTT 509C (former Devon General 509). Both carry Park Royal bodies. The AJB registrations carried on the ex-AERE Regents were in some cases retained when the vehicles were retired and transferred to members of the coach fleet.

Perched high up in the middle of Bodmin Moor is the fairly secluded village of Blisland, home of Webber's Coaches. Having just come off the Tamar Bridge, bound for Plymouth, is its former Burnley & Pendle Bristol RESL6G with a Northern Counties body, LHG 384H.

The West Country is a popular destination for holidays, and here Wallace Arnold PNW 298W, a 12-metre Leyland Leopard with a Plaxton Supreme IV body, is seen in Bretonside bus station, Plymouth, in the summer of 1981, wearing the short-lived British Coachways livery while working an express service to Birmingham.

Although a Yorkshire-based company, Wallace Arnold maintained a depot in Devon, and vehicles licensed there wore the company's original all-over cream livery. Taken the same day as the previous photograph, UNW 28M, a 12-metre Leyland Leopard with a Plaxton Panorama Elite III body, is seen in Bretonside bus station, Plymouth, with another load of happy holidaymakers.

Originally allocated to Leeds, LGL 722, a Volvo B10M-61 with a Berkhof Esprite 350 body, was transferred to Plymouth in 1987. Wearing the cream Devon livery, it is seen visiting the beautiful cathedral city of Wells on 16 August 1989. Berkhof bodies were quite rare in the Wallace Arnold fleet.

Delivered new to Wallace Arnold's Devon fleet was F445 DUG, a Volvo B10M-60 with a Plaxton Paramount 3500 III body. It was caught in Castle Way, Taunton, on 14 August 1989 at the beginning of a long journey northwards to the Orkneys. Upon retirement by Wallace Arnold in 1993, this vehicle made its home in the West Country, passing to Western National.

Pictured here in Bretonside bus station, Plymouth, in the summer of 1981 is Trathen's of Yelverton UJY 456V, a 1979 Volvo B58-61 with an Irizar Urko body – an exotic vehicle by the standards of the day! European manufacturers were beginning to appear more in UK fleets, and Trathen's was a keen user of them.

Trathen's of Yelverton also partnered National Express in the early 1980s in the development of the Rapide service between London and the West Country, having initially competed with it. Here, Van Hool Alizee-bodied Volvo B10M JSJ 430W is seen in Exeter's Paris Street coach station prior to a trip to London. Built as a demonstrator in 1980, it passed to Trathen's before returning to Scotland in 1983, shortly after this photograph was taken.

Another vehicle on the London Rapide service in Exeter that day was STT 601X, one of Trathen's fleet of Neoplan Skyliners. If memory serves, this was the service coach, with Volvo JSJ 430W working as the duplicate.

Seen here in Plymouth's Bretonside bus station on holiday tour work in the summer of 1983 is Trathen's STT 610X, a Van Hool Acron.

A slightly more unusual vehicle for an independent was LYU 542P, a Willowbrook 008 Spacecar-bodied Bedford YMT that Hookways of Meeth, in Devon, bought from National Travel South East. Seen here in Exeter's Paris Street bus station in summer 1983, it was duplicating a National Express service to Bristol.

The Devon town of Tiverton is home to Kingdom's Coaches, which bought this Willowbrook-bodied Dennis Dominator, UBG 25V, from Merseyside PTE in 1987, where it was fleet number 0025. It is pictured here on 17 August 1989 at the depot in Tiverton when in company with C212 VDD, a Dormobile-bodied Ford Transit.

Parked up in Exeter bus station was Jennings of Bude RCV 493M, a Volvo B58 with a Plaxton Elite Express III body. It is seen resting after its long run from Bude on the North Cornwall coast. Jennings always operated coaches on this service.

The village of Hemyock, on the Devon/Somerset border, was the home of Redwood's Coaches. Pictured at the depot are 108 GYC, a 1960 Bedford SB3 with a Duple Super Vega body, now preserved by the company, and FMR 503D, a Bedford SB5 with a Duple Bella Vega body bought from Barnes of Aldbourne. I have many memories of school trips and parish outings on coaches like these …

Another member of the Redwood fleet present at the depot was RNT 402H, a neat little Bedford VAS5 with a Duple Vista 25 body that was originally with the fleet of Whittle, Highley.

Berry's of Taunton is a well-known company with a major presence in Somerset's county town. I well remember seeing its smart maroon and grey coaches when I was a small boy living in Taunton. However, pictured here is one of its service buses, FBL 116K, a Bristol VRT with an ECW body. Originally 924 in the Alder Valley fleet, it was in this guise I first remember this vehicle in Reading. It is seen here in Castle Way, Taunton, on 14 August 1989 while working the bus link to the wonderful West Somerset Railway.

A typical independent's vehicle of the 1980s was Harding of Bagborough's BUX 214L, a Bedford YRT with a Duple Dominant body. It was photographed in Castle Way, Taunton, on 14 August 1989 while working the service from Wiveliscombe. This coach originated with Whittle of Highley before Harding's bought it from Bryant's of Williton.

Pictured in Castle Way, Taunton, on a private hire on 21 November 1989 is Seward's of Dalwood C304 FTT, a Bedford YNV Venturer with a Caetano Algarve body.

Weston-super-Mare is the home of Baker's Coaches, a well-known company with a history stretching back over a hundred years. Pictured in the coach park on 16 August 1989 is MED 405P, an AEC Reliance with a Duple Dominant body, one of several bought from Smith's of Wigan in 1982.

Baker's kept a few double-deckers for schools work, one of which was UGR 694R, an ECW-bodied Bristol VRT. Formerly Northumbria 515, it originated with United Automobile. It is seen in Weston-super-Mare on 16 August 1989.

Formerly Aberdeen 128, Baker's acquired this Daimler Fleetline in 1984 from Moffat & Williamson of Gauldry. Its Alexander body has been converted to single-door and it is seen in Weston-super-Mare on 16 August 1989 together with HDV 97V, a Plaxton Supreme IV Express-bodied Bedford YMT which was formerly with Phillips of Crediton.

Seen at Bath's Manvers Street bus station on 22 November 1989 is former Optare demonstrator D555 TMR, now in the fleet of Athelstan of Malmesbury, Wiltshire. An Optare City Pacer on a VW LT55 chassis, it represents the second, more stylish, generation of purpose-built minibuses, as opposed to the so-called 'bread vans'.

Reversing out of Manvers Street bus station, Bath, on 22 November 1989 is BDF 205Y, an ECW-bodied Leyland Tiger TRCTL11/3R that was previously in the National Travel fleet. Purchased by L. Munden of Bristol in 1988, it is heading for the village of East Harptree. This vehicle later found its way to Wake's and received a new East Lancs body.

Grey Cars was the coaching arm of Devon General. It was combined with the Greenslades name and eventually disappeared, but was revived during the 1980s when Devon General sold its coach operations in 1987. D39 HMT, a Van Hool Alizee-bodied Leyland Royal Tiger in the ownership of Bruce-Robertson of Torquay, displays an update of the old Grey Cars livery. It is seen in Bath on 22 November 1989.

Parked up in Weston-super-Mare on 16 August 1989 was 666 VHU from the fleet of Bevan, Edge End, near Lydney in the Forest of Dean, which traded under the name of Dukes Travel. Previously registered OKY 85R, this 12-metre Leyland Leopard with a Plaxton Supreme body was new to National Travel East and it found its way to Gloucestershire to live via Regan of Worthing and Eagle of Bristol.

Seen laying over in Cheltenham's Royal Well bus station is TUO 85J, a Willowbrook-bodied AEC Reliance from the fleet of Jones Bros of Malvern. A former Devon General vehicle, it was purchased by Jones Bros in June 1981, passing to Crump of Malvern in 1984.

Caught the same day as the Jones AEC was another Reliance, this time with a Plaxton Supreme Express body, bought new by Marchant's of Cheltenham. A well-established operator of over sixty years, Marchant's was a keen user of AECs, both new and second-hand, in both bus and coach forms.

Photographed in Cheltenham's Royal Well bus station during a 1983 visit is LFH 719V, a Leyland Leopard with a Plaxton Supreme IV Express body. Wearing the all-black livery of the Castleways fleet, it is seen awaiting departure back to its home village of Winchcombe.

Cottrell's of Mitcheldean was a small operator working into Gloucester from Ruardean and Cinderford in the Forest of Dean. It always had a small number of double-deckers in the fleet, purchasing them both new and second-hand. A second-hand example, GBU 6V is formerly Greater Manchester PTE MCW Metrobus 5006, one of three that Cottrell's bought. It is seen leaving Gloucester bus station for Cinderford on 11 July 1987 – a service which Cottrell's took over from National Welsh in 1985.

Caught on the same day leaving Gloucester bus station for Ruardean was Cottrell's immaculate Northern Counties-bodied Leyland Fleetline EAD 122T. This was the last new double-decker bought by Cottrell's. A Swanbrook Bedford/Plaxton can be seen parked in the background.

Swanbrook of Cheltenham bought HKJ 255N, a Bedford YRQ with a Willowbrook body, from Maidstone Borough Council in June 1980. Lasting in the fleet until 1989, it is seen here leaving Gloucester bus station on 11 July 1987.

Bristol REs were popular purchases with independent operators in the 1980s. Parfitt of Rhymney Bridge in South Wales purchased former East Midland NNN 7M, a Bristol RELH6L with an ECW body, in September 1989 and immediately showed it off at the Showbus Rally held at Woburn Abbey on 24 September 1989. This vehicle has since been preserved in its original East Midland NBC livery.

Delivered in 1988 to Thomas of Tonypandy in Mid-Glamorgan as E334 PWO, this DAF SBR3000 with a Berkhof Excellence 2000HD body was eventually registered as F334 YTG. It is seen here in Weston-super-Mare on 16 August 1989.

The Leyland Royal Tiger was a top-of-the-range coach chassis fitted with a Roe Doyen coach body. This combination even inspired a piece of music called 'Doyen' by the well-known brass band composer Goff Richards, premiered by the Leyland Band at the vehicle's launch. This example in the Warners Fairfax fleet was new in 1984 as B602 MDG, being reregistered 6017 WF in 1987. It is pictured outside its garage in Tewkesbury on 11 July 1987.

Another coach in the Warners fleet photographed on 11 July 1987 was 9246 WF. Previously registered VWX 295X, then EBW 44A, it is a Leyland Tiger with a Plaxton Supreme IV body that Warners bought from Wallace Arnold in 1987.

Moving up into the West Midlands, we find Mid-Warwickshire Motors of Balsall Common and their YAY 701J parked in Coventry's Pool Meadow bus station sometime around 1981. It is a Daimler Fleetline with a Willowbrook body purchased from the Road Transport Industry Training Board. It survived in the fleet until about 1984.

Purchased in March 1981 from Garelochhead Coach Services as Duple Dominant-bodied bus TGD 218R, Stevenson's of Spath in Staffordshire rebodied this Leyland Leopard with a Plaxton Paramount 3200 II body in 1985 and reregistered it 961 PEH. Pictured here at the depot in Spath in 1987, it survived in the fleet until 1991.

Another member of Stevenson's coach fleet was DEN 247W, a Volvo B58-61 with a Plaxton Supreme IV body. Originally in the Lancashire United fleet, it was purchased from Greater Manchester PTE in 1985. Bearing the name of the Viking coaching subsidiary, it is seen on a private hire to Weston-super-Mare on 16 August 1989.

Stevenson's took the opportunity to display its brand-new G109 YRE, a Scania K93CRB fitted with Alexander PS body, at the Showbus Rally, Woburn Abbey, on 24 September 1989.

British Independent Buses in the 1980s 49

Stevenson's expanded its fleet by buying a large number of London's unwanted DMS type Daimler Fleetlines, such as Park Royal-bodied JGF 298K, seen here in 1986 in Uttoxeter bus station. Previously DMS 298, it has been converted to single-door, as were all the DMS types bought by Stevenson's.

This very smart Alexander Y Type-bodied Leyland Leopard was bought from Lancaster City Council in March 1984, in whose fleet it was numbered 18. MFR 18P is also seen in Uttoxeter bus station in 1986.

Captured in 1986 in Derby bus station is Berresford's of Cheddleton SWL 49J. Bought in 1981 from City of Oxford Motor Services, it is an AEC Reliance with a Willowbrook body, and is seen carrying the 'Derbyman' name for the company's Manchester to Derby service. Sadly, this interesting operator is another one that is no longer with us, ceasing operations in 1987.

Hulley's of Baslow operated through the beautiful Derbyshire Peak District. It developed a liking for Bristol REs, operating a number of them, including this former Trent example, YCH 896M, which was purchased in May 1989. A RELH6L with an ECW coach body, Hulley's took the opportunity to show it off at the Showbus Rally at Woburn Abbey on 24 September 1989, where I managed to capture it. It stayed in the fleet until 1991.

Another Bristol RE in Hulley's fleet, this time with Silver Service fleet names, was PCW 202J, an ex-Burnley & Pendle RESL6L with Pennine bodywork. It was captured in the mid-1980s in Bakewell. REs with Pennine bodies were never a common combination.

Also seen in Bakewell on that day was KWE 144P, a Bedford YRT with a Duple Dominant Express body bought new in 1975.

Pictured here when almost new on a tour to Devon is Barratt's of Nantwich ADM 774W, a Ford R1114 with a Duple Dominant IV body. It is parked in Paris Street coach station in Exeter while its passengers explore the delights of this lovely cathedral city.

Mayne of Clayton, near Manchester, entered its brand-new Plaxton Supreme IV-bodied Leyland Leopard HDB 354V in the Brighton Coach Rally on 20 April 1980.

After buying AEC Regent Vs and then Daimler Fleetlines, Maynes of Clayton developed a liking for ECW-bodied Bristol VRTs, like VJA 667S. Fitted with coach seats, it is seen on a private hire to York in the early 1980s, despite the destination blind saying it's bound for Clayton on route 209!

LWM 475G from the Smiths of Wigan fleet was delivered in 1969 with a Duple (Northern) Commander III body. It was rebodied with this Duple Dominant II body in 1981 and is seen here in Dawlish soon after on a tour to Paignton.

Yelloway's NNC 855P, a Duple Dominant-bodied AEC Reliance, leaves Cheltenham for Leeds on route 223 on a return journey from the West Country in about 1983.

Yelloway is probably best remembered for its express services from Rochdale to the South West. Here, Plaxton Supreme-bodied AEC Reliance SBU 303R is seen leaving Cheltenham for Rochdale on its return run from Paignton in about 1983.

One of the last batch of AEC Reliances delivered to Yelloway in 1979, Plaxton Supreme IV-bodied WDK 564T is seen in Drummer Street bus station, Cambridge, bound for Rochdale from Clacton – a service worked jointly with Premier Travel. Photographed in the early 1980s, one of Premier Travel's Alexander-bodied AEC Reliances can be seen in the background.

Captured at the Brighton Coach Rally on 21 April 1984 is A336 WCA, a brand-new Duple Caribbean-bodied Leyland Tiger of Bostock, Congleton. Delivered in April 1984, this could well have been its first outing!

Leyland, near Preston, was the home of J. Fishwick & Sons, whose smart two-tone green vehicles were a regular sight around Preston. Being based in Leyland meant that Leylands were a natural choice for the company. Here, Leyland Lynx D25 VCW is seen laying over in Preston's large bus station in October 1988.

A trip to Glasgow for an orchestral audition presented the opportunity to photograph a number of operators in this city. Here, A1 Services' SCS 384M, a Volvo B58 with a Duple Dominant body, leaves Glasgow's Buchanan bus station on 28 June 1989, bound for Ardrossan.

British Independent Buses in the 1980s 57

Seen parked next to a Clydeside Scottish Dennis Dorchester in Buchanan bus station on 28 June 1989 is A1 Services' MTV 753P, a Leyland Leopard with a Duple Dominant E Type body that A1 bought from Nottingham City Transport. The E Type body was a Duple Dominant coach body, but fitted with bus seats and sliding vents in the windows.

St Vincent Place, Glasgow, on 28 June 1989 was the venue for Wilson's of Carnwath YTB 944N, a Bristol RESL6G with an East Lancs body purchased from Hyndburn Transport.

Photographed in Renfrew Street, Glasgow, on 28 June 1989, was NFB 598R. New to the Bristol Omnibus Company as its 3030, this Leyland National had made its way to the fleet of Green, Kirkintilloch, via Kerfoot-Davies of Dyserth. Displaying a Strathclyde Transport sticker in its windscreen, it is working route 70 to Waterside.

Dodds of Troon was the owner of RCS 713R, a Seddon Pennine 7 with an Alexander T Type body that it purchased from Western SMT in 1988. It is seen here leaving Buchanan bus station, Glasgow, on 29 June 1989. It survived in the fleet until 1993.

British Independent Buses in the 1980s 59

Resting in Buchanan bus station, Glasgow, on 28 June 1989, before setting off on its 138-mile journey to Campbeltown is West Coast Motors E360 XSB, a Volvo B10M-61 with a Plaxton Paramount 3500 III body.

While Leyland Nationals were not that common in Scotland, one operator that did seem to like them was McGill's of Barrhead. Seen here leaving Glasgow's Buchanan bus station on 29 June 1989 is DYS 637T.

McGill's bought both Mark 1 and Mark 2 versions of the Leyland National. Pictured leaving Buchanan bus station on 28 June 1989 while bound for Barrhead is UGE 388W, a Mark 2 model with the front-mounted radiator.

Seen here on Renfrew Street, Glasgow, on 28 June 1989 is Hutchison of Overtown D888 PGA, an integral Duple 425. I recall riding on Alder Valley's 'Londonlink' examples of these coaches and found them very comfortable and speedy!

Cotter's Tours of Glasgow entered its month-old NSU 632V in the 1980 Brighton Coach Rally, held on 20 April. A Volvo B58-61 with a Van Hool Aragon body, it is seen here undergoing driving tests on the Madeira Drive. This firm also competed with both National Express and British Coachways on the London to Glasgow route, but ceased operations in 1987.

York Pullman's smart, distinctive livery has graced the streets of York and the surrounding area for many years. Here, its Bedford YRT PDN 209M, with a Plaxton Elite Express III body, is seen in the city loading for a trip to Linton sometime in the early 1980s.

Photographed from the city walls in the mid-1980s, York Pullman's HVY 132X, a Bedford YMT with a Plaxton Bustler body, is seen on Fossbank, York.

Now part of the York Pullman group, Wray's of Harrogate is an old family firm dating back to the 1920s. Captured in Park Lane, London, in the mid-1980s on a private hire is its GUA 794Y, a Volvo B10M-61 with a Plaxton Paramount 3200 that was delivered in February 1983.

Pictured in Sheffield's Pond Street bus station in 1987 is Wigmore of Dinnington UKY 608Y, a Bedford YMT with Duple Dominant bus bodywork.

Caught in Rosemary Street, Mansfield, is Maun's Bristol VRTSL RKB 98N (formerly Merseyside 2098), which is fitted with an East Lancs body. Pictured in 1987 heading for Sutton, it was eventually scrapped in 1990.

A parental move to near Nottingham in 1983 brought the opportunity to photograph fleets in the East Midlands. Parked in Newark bus station sometime in 1985 is Wright's of Newark PRR 89M, a Volvo B58-56 with a Duple Dominant Express body. It is seen shortly before departing for Ollerton, a village north-west of Newark.

A well-known operator in Nottinghamshire was Gash of Newark, whose BR2, HRB 848N, a Bristol LHS6L with angular Marshall bodywork, is seen here in 1985 in Newark bus station. Gash eventually sold out, in 1989, to Lincolnshire Road Car.

Parked in Newark bus station is GVO 839N, numbered L12 in the Gash fleet. A Plaxton Derwent-bodied Leyland Leopard, it is seen prior to departure for Bingham during 1987.

Gash's DD13 (TWH 811K) was a 33-foot East Lancs-bodied Leyland Atlantean purchased from Greater Manchester PTE in August 1984. A far cry from the fleet of half-cab Daimler double-deckers for which Gash was well-known, it is seen here in 1987 in Newark bus station.

Photographed very hastily near Nottingham's Broadmarsh bus station is Gash of Newark DD12 (JUS 784N). Purchased from Greater Glasgow PTE, where it was LA937, in November 1982, this Leyland Atlantean with panoramic Alexander bodywork stayed with Gash until it was scrapped in 1989.

South Notts was an old established operator operating regular services into Nottingham and the surrounding area with its fleet of distinctive dark blue double-deckers. Arriving in Loughborough from Nottingham is WJN 352J, a Northern Counties-bodied Daimler Fleetline bought from Southend Transport. This company was later sold to Nottingham City Transport.

Skills of Nottingham is a well-known and long established business whose distinctive pale green coaches were a familiar sight all over the country on excursions and tours. Seen in the somewhat spartan King's Cross coach station in 1982 is MRA 65W, a 12-metre Leyland Leopard with a Plaxton Supreme IV body.

Radcliffe-on-Trent was the home of Lamcote's Coaches, which purchased this Alexander-bodied Leyland Atlantean from Tyne & Wear PTE in July 1980. SVK 613G stayed in the fleet until 1989 and is seen here at the company's depot.

Purchased from the Devon Area Health Authority in 1977, this Willowbrook-bodied Ford R192, UOD 433J, is captured at the Lamcote depot during the same visit. It stayed in the fleet until 1989.

The four villages near Nottingham where my father was appointed rector in 1983 were served by Barton, and one of those villages, Plungar, had a Barton outstation. Parked there on 29 March 1987 was their 1375 (OAL 619M), a Leyland Leopard with a Plaxton Elite Express III body. Part of the large fleet of bus-grant bodied coaches bought in the 1970s and 1980s to standardise the fleet, which was then quite varied, this vehicle found its way to Ireland upon withdrawal from the Barton fleet before being scrapped in 1998.

Another one of the large influx of grant-aided vehicles into the Barton fleet was their 501 (RCH 501R), a Plaxton Supreme Express-bodied Leyland Leopard. It is pictured here around 1985 in Loughborough bus station. Barton merged with the neighbouring Trent company in 1989.

Photographed in Loughborough bus station in 1985, shortly before its sale, is Howlett's of Quorn 77 (XAY 275S), a Plaxton Supreme Express-bodied Leyland Leopard.

Seen entering Grantham bus station sometime in 1984 is WGR 848R, a Plaxton Derwent-bodied Leyland Leopard purchased by Reliance of Great Gonerby from Trimdon Motor Services in 1983.

Another operator I got to photograph on these parental visits was Appleby's. A 1985 visit to its Grimsby depot revealed these three Plaxton-bodied vehicles: GCN 496N, a Bedford YRQ with a Panorama Elite III body, was bought from Nicolson of Burnley; OPT 92J, a Leyland Leopard also with a Panorama Elite III body (which was fitted in 1981 after fire damage to its original Plaxton body), was bought from Body of Bridlington in 1982; and TTL 541R, a Bedford YMT with a Supreme Express body, was bought new.

Grimsby depot also revealed a former Greater Glasgow PTE Leyland Atlantean with the usual Alexander body, KSU 853P. Formerly LA 977, it is seen here parked among native Appleby Plaxton-bodied Bedfords.

Appleby's DFW 782X, a Bedford YNT with a Plaxton Supreme V body, is another vehicle photographed at the bleak King's Cross coach station.

Limbs of Maltby in South Yorkshire bought TPJ 286S from Bexleyheath Transport in 1982. A Bedford YMT with a Duple Dominant II body, it is seen in 1988 in Bressenden Place, London, on a private hire.

Caught in King's Lynn bus station during its brief stay with Swaffham Coachways is former London DMS Fleetline MLK 563L. During its London days it was allocated to Putney Garage for a while, and I rode on it a few times as it worked service 85 past my college.

Premier Travel's distinctive two-tone blue livery was a familiar sight around Cambridge for many years. Pictured here parked in Drummer Street bus station in 1981 is OJE 550M, one of its well-known Alexander-bodied AEC Reliances.

After buying Alexander-bodied AECs for many years, Premier Travel turned to Plaxton from 1975 onwards. Seen in Drummer Street bus station, Cambridge, is NEB 346R, which was part of the 1976 delivery and one of the second batch to carry Plaxton Supreme Express bodies. Seen on a local service, this vehicle stayed in the fleet until 1989, when it was bought by the Forestry Commission.

Premier Travel exhibited its WEB 408T, an AEC Reliance with a Plaxton Supreme IV Express body, at the Showbus '80 Rally at Thorpe Park, near Staines. This vehicle stayed in the fleet until 1995.

When production of the AEC Reliance ceased, Premier Travel turned to the manual gearbox Leyland Leopard. Here, number 286 (BVA 788V), fitted with a Plaxton Supreme IV Express body, is seen in Drummer Street bus station, Cambridge, on a local bus service to Fulbourne.

Premier Travel's D524 LCS was the first Volvo it operated, having had the vehicle on loan prior to purchase. Fitted with a Plaxton Paramount 3200 II body, it is seen here in the late 1980s while sporting a new, predominantly silver livery, in Park Lane, London, on a private hire.

Whippet of Fenstanton has been a familiar sight around the Cambridge/Huntingdon/St Ives area since 1919. Seen here soon after delivery in 1980 in Drummer Street bus station, Cambridge, while preparing to depart for St Ives is EAV 811V, a Northern Counties-bodied Leyland Atlantean.

Whippet quite frequently used members of its coach fleet on its bus services, as shown here by CAV 626V, a Volvo B58 with a Duple Dominant II Express body. It was photographed in 1980 when very new in Drummer Street bus station, Cambridge.

While London may not have liked the DMS class of Daimler Fleetlines, getting rid of its large fleet prematurely, they did go on to serve other operators very efficiently. Cooks of Biggleswade purchased MLK 439L, a Park Royal-bodied example, in the early 1980s. It is seen here in 1984 in Baldock High Street on the service to Stevenage.

The Colchester area has long been an interesting district for independent bus operation. Here, JRT 710N, a Bedford YRT with a Plaxton Derwent body belonging to Chambers of Bures, is seen in company with Osborne's of Tollesbury LWC 445V, a Bedford YMT with a Plaxton Supreme IV Express body, in Colchester bus station in 1986.

Chambers of Bures standardised on Bedfords for many years. Seen here in Colchester bus station in 1986 is WDX 396X, a YMT with a Duple Dominant bus body.

Osborne's of Tollesbury operated into Colchester from its base in Essex. Pictured here in 1986, together with previously seen LWC445V and an unidentified Bova is MWW 759K (formerly West Yorkshire 1366), a Bristol RELL6G with an ECW body.

Caught on the same day as its Bristol RE was Osborne's RTW 148R, a Bedford YMT with a Duple Dominant Express body that was bought new by the company.

Seen here in 1985 is Osborne's LJT 939P, a Bristol LH6L with an ECW body that started life with Hants & Dorset as its 3806. Osborne's bought it in 1983, selling it on to Trimdon Motor Services in 1988.

A few miles from Colchester, on the road to Sudbury, is the village of Nayland, home to Norfolk's of Nayland. Photographed in 1988 in its garage is TWX 193L (formerly West Yorkshire 1371), a Bristol RELL6G with an ECW body. In the back of the garage can be seen similar NWU 324M (previously West Yorkshire 1399) and Plaxton Supreme IV-bodied Volvo B58 90 NOR, which was new as NPV 444W.

Caught in Colchester bus station in 1985 is Norfolk's former West Midlands 3978 (SOE 978H), a Park Royal-bodied Daimler Fleetline. It is seen while bound for Great Horkesley, a small village just north of Colchester.

A unique vehicle was Hedingham & District's L81 (YNO 481L), the only Marshall Camair-bodied Bedford YRT built. It is seen here leaving Colchester bus station in 1985, heading for Chappel. Sadly this vehicle did not survive as it was destroyed by fire.

Laying over in Colchester bus station in 1988 with L81 is Hedingham's L95 (JAR 495V), a Duple Dominant bus-bodied Bedford YLQ. Hedingham's purchases were always a mixture of new and carefully chosen second-hand vehicles.

In 1982, Hedingham & District purchased all four of Eastern National's ECW-bodied Bristol LHs. Pictured here is L113 (UVX 6S). They survived much longer with Hedingham, remaining in service until 1999.

Purchased in 1982 was BAR 103X, which was numbered L103 in the Hedingham fleet. Seen here laying over in Colchester bus station in 1988 next to Bristol LH L113, it was a Leyland Leopard with Plaxton Bustler body.

Hedingham & District bought its only Leyland Lynx, L150 (F150 LTW), in 1988. On 24 September 1989 the company displayed it at the Showbus Rally held at Woburn Abbey.

British Independent Buses in the 1980s 83

Pictured at Showbus, Woburn Abbey, on 24 September 1989 is HCS 804N from the fleet of Sworder, Walkern, near Stevenage. New to Western SMT as its L2519, this Alexander-bodied Leyland Leopard joined the Sworder fleet in late 1987, remaining there until 1994.

Seamarks of Luton developed a liking for DAF vehicles and purchased quite a number over the years. Pictured at the somewhat primitive King's Cross coach station is VBM 716W, a DAF MB200 with a Plaxton Supreme IV body that joined the fleet as its 174 in May 1981. It lasted in service with the company until April 1985.

A lot of independent operators chose to standardise on particular makes, while others operated a wide variety of different types. Buffalo of Flitwick in Bedfordshire was of the latter group, and a number of its vehicles were in use at the Showbus '89 Rally, held at Woburn Abbey on 24 September, on services for the visitors. This group of photographs will show something of the variety to be found in the Buffalo fleet at this time. In this shot, JPA 171K (formerly Green Line RP71), a Park Royal-bodied AEC Reliance, is pictured.

Illustrated here is CKC 328L (formerly Merseyside PTE 3028), an MCW-bodied Daimler Fleetline. Although based in Bedfordshire, Buffalo operated some contracts on behalf of Hertfordshire County Council, as shown by the notice in the windscreen.

A relatively youthful second-hand addition to the Buffalo fleet was HDB 437V (formerly Greater Manchester PTE 1437), a Northern Counties-bodied Dennis Dominator that found its way to Bedfordshire via the fleet of Whippet, Fenstanton.

Buffalo also bought new vehicles, including F151 KGS, which was one of three Plaxton Derwent-bodied Volvo B10Ms purchased in 1988.

At the same time as the Volvo saloons, Buffalo bought two relatively rare Leyland Swifts with Wadham Stringer Vanguard bodies. F154 KGS is pictured here.

Aylesbury in Buckinghamshire was the home of Red Rover. Pictured on the main A325 Farnborough Road while bringing a party to the Farnborough Air Show in 1984 is FJO 143V, a Bedford YMT with a Caetano Alpha body. Red Rover did not survive the 1980s, passing to Luton & District, part of the former United Counties company, in 1988.

Tappins of Wallingford bought MBO 512F from Cardiff Corporation, where it was fleet number 512, in 1980. An Alexander-bodied AEC Swift, it is seen at its garage in Didcot in 1981. It has since been preserved in South Wales in its original Cardiff livery.

Seen on the same day as the AEC Swift are Tappins' CBK 502C and CBK 504C, Bedford SB13s with Plaxton Embassy bodies. These two vehicles were new to Byng's of Portsmouth.

A more up-to-date Bedford in the Tappins fleet was URD 32S. Photographed at the Showbus '80 rally at Thorpe Park, near Staines, it is a Plaxton Supreme-bodied Bedford YMT.

A well-known operator in the Reading area was Chiltern Queens, from Woodcote, just over the border into Oxfordshire. YNX 478 was a particularly interesting vehicle. New in 1958 with a Duple Britannia body, this AEC Reliance was bought by Chiltern Queens in 1970. In 1973 it was rebodied with this 1956 Duple Midland body from 530 BPG, a rare Dennis Pelican that the company bought in 1962. It is pictured here at Reading station in 1982, the year I bought the Ford Fiesta seen in the background.

New to Somerset independent Hutchings & Cornelius of South Petherton, TYD 122G arrived with Chiltern Queens in September 1980 after spending about a year with Tillingbourne. An AEC Reliance with a Willowbrook body, it is seen at Reading station on 22 April 1989 and survives in preservation.

Over the years Chiltern Queens has bought a number of vehicles from City of Oxford Motor Services. One of these vehicles was TJO 53K, an AEC Reliance with a Marshall body. It is seen here at Reading station while setting off on a journey back to its base at Woodcote on 30 October 1989.

New to the fleet in 1972, Chiltern Queens' EUD 256K, seen here at Reading station on 31 October 1989, is an AEC Reliance with a Plaxton Derwent body. Parked behind it is three-month-old Optare StarRider F986 TTF, which is still to receive fleet livery. Happily, EUD is now preserved at the Oxford Bus Museum.

Another independent operator working into Reading was House of Watlington, recognisable by the distinctive red and orange livery. Photographed on Station Hill, Reading, in 1985 is EWL 771V, a Ford R1114 with Plaxton Supreme IV Express bodywork that stayed in the fleet until 1987.

Deregulation in the mid-1980s led to a colourful period in the former London Transport area, with a number of independent operators taking over former red bus routes as they were offered out on franchise. The 81 service to Slough from Hounslow saw the arrival of the yellow buses of London Buslines, represented here in the shape of D751 DLO – a Leyland Lynx caught at Slough bus station on 30 October 1989. London Buslines was run by coach operator Len Wright. It was taken over by Centrewest in 1996 and eventually became part of First Group.

Moore of Windsor, who traded as Imperial, operated a local service in Windsor. In 1980 it bought JHL 318P, a Bedford YRQ with a Willowbrook body, from Mowbray of Stanley. It is seen here in the mid-1980s outside Windsor Castle. It survived in the fleet until 1987.

Tellings Golden Miller of Byfleet resurrected the Glenton Tours name and livery in the late 1980s. Seen here parked at The Hard in Portsmouth on 27 May 1989 is two-month-old Volvo B10M F805 TMD. Its Van Hool Alizee body was very different from the centre-entrance Plaxton bodies carried by the original Glenton Tours vehicles.

Another operator to take advantage of London's early disposal of its DMS Daimler Fleetlines was Windsorian, who bought MLH 304L, an MCW-bodied example, in 1980. Converting it to open-top, it operated it on a sightseeing tour around Windsor. It is seen here outside Windsor Castle in around 1981.

A major Central London bus route to fall into the hands of an independent operator in the 1980s was the 24, from Chalk Farm to Pimlico. It passed to Grey Green, the well-known coach operator, in 1988. A batch of Alexander-bodied Volvo Citybuses was purchased for the route and number 142 (F142 PHM) is seen here on Victoria Street on 2 November 1989. London became quite a colourful place during this period, until it became a requirement for all buses to be predominantly red.

The Round London Sightseeing Tour is very popular, and has produced some interesting vehicles over the years. In use on this work in 1984 was KTF 591, belonging to Ebdon of Sidcup. A 1949 AEC Regent III with Park Royal bodywork, it was purchased from Lancaster City Council by Ebdon in December 1983, having originated with Morecambe & Heysham Corporation before its merger with Lancaster in 1974. It is seen in Grosvenor Place, near Victoria station.

Caught at the same time and same location, and in total contrast to the venerable AEC, is Ebdon's GVL 939Y, a very stylish Neoplan Skyliner, engaged on similar work.

London Cityrama was another operator engaged on sightseeing work in the capital and its bright blue buses were a familiar sight on the streets. On this work in 1984 was LLH 6K, a Roe-bodied Leyland Atlantean. Seen here in Buckingham Palace Road, I believe this vehicle was initially used on BOAC journeys to Heathrow Airport when new.

Metrobus has its origins in the Tillingbourne company in Surrey, having started life as Tillingbourne Metropolitan. Nowadays it is a large company and part of the Go-Ahead Group. However, in 1986 it was still a small independent operator, with a fleet of twenty-four vehicles in November of that year. Pictured here outside the Fairfield Halls in Croydon – reckoned by some to be the best concert hall in London – is WKE 67S, a Duple Dominant-bodied Bedford YMT purchased in 1985 from Maidstone Borough Council. In this picture it is working service 357 to Orpington.

Ending where we started in Guildford with Safeguard we see D159 HML, a Mercedes-Benz 609D with Reeve Burgess a body that was purchased in April 1987. Seen here entering Guildford Friary bus station on a local service, it was an ideal vehicle for negotiating some of the smaller, congested roads on the estates around Guildford.

Bibliography

Burnett, George and Laurie James, *The Tillingbourne Bus Story* (Midhurst: Middleton Press, 1990).

James, Laurie, *Safeguard Coaches of Guildford* (Stroud: Amberley Publishing, 2014).

James, Laurie, *Somerset's Buses* (Stroud: Tempus Publishing, 2004).

Peto, A. W., D. J. Stanier and D. Pelington, *Stevensons of Uttoxeter* (Burton-on-Trent: J. M. Pearson, 1984).

Richmond, Roy and Andrew Richmond, *Epsom Coaches* (Croydon: DTS Publishing, 2002).